Rhythmic Love, Treble Heartbreak

April J. Sydnor

Copyright © 2012 Rhythmic Love, Treble Heartbreak by April J. Sydnor
Cover designed by Lindsey E. Bates
All rights reserved. This book may not be reproduced in whole or in part (except in the case of reviews) without written permission from the author.
ISBN-10: 0615652662
ISBN-13: 978-0615652665

Printed in the United States of America

TO: MY HEART

Thanks for writing, listening, thinking, rapping, singing, praying, cursing, laughing, crying, promising, dreaming, believing and loving unapologetically.

Intro(spective)duction

Growing up, we think of love in beautifully fragmented images – kaleidoscope impressions. We view love through auto self-correcting lenses, seeing only its perfection. Life rips these glasses off with an abrupt yank. Still, we walk on wooden planks, blindfolded and handcuffed, to the edge of the cliff. Willing to leap into the outstretched arms of love. Still seeking that flawless entity. It takes several semesters of studying Shakespearean tragedies and listening to the radio in nighttime solitude to even fathom effacing love's misconception. We begin to understand its raw nature – the beauty of love is inherent in its imperfections. There is truth nestled in the pain. Tears bring us face to face with the hurt. Sometimes the dirt can be seen for what it is: escape. There are times when our watercolor faith in love is superseded only by the Disney princesses coloring book innocence we take for granted. Trust rusts in our pockets one heartbreak at a time. Soon enough we find comfort in the tone of our xylophone tears. Even sooner we gain origami confidence in love. It creates this habit of romanticizing hopelessly. Hoping we, can find solace in those clasped hands and the sounds escaping our headphones. After being in love with Love for all the wrong reasons, seasons change and I grow. I know about putting every organ into loving someone the way they deserve to be. To me, it's the honesty in our emotions that breathe life into loving. Loving feels like hearing your favorite song – the first and last time simultaneously. Herein lays the perfection of love – the feeling it evokes. That perfect combination of music and lyrics, verses and beats. This rhythm in my heart. Rhythmic Love, Treble Heartbreak.

CONTENTS

Xylophone Education - The Cliché Puppy Love Romance
- Windy City Sorta Love — Page # 8
- Crayolas and Sharpies — 9
- Firsts — 11
- Let's Play — 13
- Virgin Thought — 15
- Love Is... — 17

Silent Cymbals, Clashing
- Void — 20
- Broken Rhyme — 22
- Disney — 24
- We Need — 26
- Morning After — 29
- Rebirth — 31

Rhythmic Love
- Convinced... Love — 34
- Brown Sugar — 36
- In His Image — 37
- Untold Story — 39
- Imperfect Conversation — 41
- Pronoun's Love — 43
- School Subjects — 46
- Class In Session — 48
- Poem Speak — 50

Bass Blaring Headphones, Failing Organs, Screaming Lyrics, Crying Violins, Treble Heartbreak
- Five Reasons for Apologies — 53
- Letting Go of Safe — 55
- These Days Lately — 57
- Love DeLorean — 59
- Guilt and Tears — 61
- Losing Religion — 63

- If Only You Knew   66

Seven Day Forecast – Rain Tapped Percussion
- Sunrise   72
- March Madness   74
- A... Typical Storm   76
- Music   78
- Soulmate/ Stormy Weather   80
- Abstract Complexity   84

Love; The Finale

Phase One	Love Knot	87
Phase Two....................	Love Transformation	89
Phase Three.................	Love Suicides	91
Happy Ending...............	Two Words ... One Love	94

I.

Xylophone Education -The Cliché Puppy Love Romance

Windy City Sorta Love

And, I always told you
We got a Chicago style love
As doves, we fly through the night sky and survey the landscape from above
Leave my John Hancock on your Sears Tower of a frame
When lame you carried. Me,
Headaches from dead weight. Buried
Heartbreak in the urban ghetto
Bandaged heads wrapped like turbans
Stiletto stair climbed from the Redline platform... to heaven
Leavened bread intoxicates our bodies while in the midst of ...you know.
Chicago weather turns from wet to wetter, then mist and you snow
You show up sunlight bright on cloudy days
Rainbow rays on any "L"
Well, did I ever tell you
    We got a deep dish kinda love
All the sauciness on top, stuffed with your favorite toppings
    Magnificent Mile Shopping
This love reminds me of gentrification
Replacing hoodies with cardigans
We bought out dilapidated cardiac and displaced the hurt
Now all I know is art be at, where pain was at first

Crayolas and Sharpies

I think,
Back in kindergarten, when the more colorful the page the prettier it seemed
I must've daydreamed
Of a winter garden, with a sky
Cerulean
Where we were one with the stars, just me and you
A Valentine's Day flower
Carnation Pink and Blue
...Sitting on the clouds puts the irrelevance of fast cars
In perspective
Reflective
Of learning the alphabet and numbers
The backdrop of the white paper to pencil lead, the lumber
Sometimes my pillow's wet, a slumber
Traveled to in the midst of bedtime stories and being tucked in at night
Awaiting day break
On half days
I colored the Sun yellow and orange, barely staying within the lines
On the page, glitter
Littered my mind's recesses
I remember at recess, I ran from a boy tryin' to kiss me
Innocent young Ms. Me
In a sense, I missed
We,
Could be happily ever after by now.
Somehow
At that age friendships were contingent on having similar favorite colors
Mines was violet
I don't remember my best friend's
I guess when
We get older, it no longer matters

About nineteen years later

I take out my black Sharpie and sign your chest
Really hoping the felt tip touches through and leaves my signature on the inside
At least you know I tried
At least you know I love you sincerely
We got a BFF chained and blowtorched link
After all, I made sure I'm on your heart in permanent ink

FIRSTS

He was the first man I ever cared so deeply about
And the first time a kiss meant so much
This being the first time I let a man touch
My heart
In such a way
So this was the first time I heard a man say
"I love you" in this way
Naturally
This was a time, all I could do is pray
That times like this would last forever,
So forever and a day has come and gone
And yesterday was the last day I cried to the song
Of my tears
...But he was the first man that tasted my tears
And kissed the sorrow away, so that even after tomorrow it'd stay
Locked up somewhere
And I still care
And I still dare, to love again
'Cause once again
He was the first man I ever had these feelings for
And the first time I had opened that door
This being the first time I knew what was in store
But was hesitant to approach it
Finding and losing focus
In those eyes
Those were the first eyes that looked at me with a gaze so intense
I felt a passionate suspense
In his presence
In his essence
...I often found myself lost
And even now, I don't know if the cost,
Could suffice
He was nice
..And good to me
His hands were the first to feel so familiar

And being so familiar resulted in feelings of ecstasy
A pleasantry
That makes it hard to forget
That he was the first man I let
In my heart
He was the first man to break my heart
This is the first time I don't know where or how to start
To move on
Truth is, he's gone
And left without a warning
A goodbye
Clouds storming
I still cry
He was the first to love
And last to try
To heal my heart
It hurts because I wasn't the first and won't be the last in his repertoire,
And I feel scars
And I care more
And I wear more
Than my emotions on my sleeve
I know I'll be the first and last to grieve
Because
He was
And still is
Kinda special
Though he didn't and still doesn't deserve to be
He looked at me
And for the first time I was speechless
Regardless
This is the first time I'm writing my last poem about that special someone
I'm trying but my will gets weak and I feel so numb,
Because
He was the first man I ever cared so deeply about

Let's Play

...Let's play pretend
Like sin is the end
And start of a new beginnin'
Let's get a needle and thread to mend
Our hearts
Let's start spinnin'
A web
Where we wait and catch what we need
Let's take a house deed
From the game of Life,
Some Monopoly Money, and start a life
You can land on the square that says get a wife
And pick me
Let's take a Chance
And a ride on the Reading
Let's start reading
Fairytales,
Might as well,
Be a happily ever after on 79th street
Let's play hide and seek...
In the dark,
Let's play on swings, in the park
And jump out at the highest peak,
In the midst of Mr. Freeze
Let's run into the future far ahead of everybody else
Let's be the ones who shuffled and dealt
Their dirty hearts
Around
Knowing
Eventually they'd be growing,
As a rock teacher
I plan on showing
You, why I'm the queen of spades
Let's find some sunny shade
And sit there
Let's wear
Costumes

...I'll be you and you'll be me
That way we both can know how it feels to love each other perfectly

Virgin Thought

They say the greatest gift is chastity
But there has to be
More to it than this
Reminisce
About the purity of a kiss
Upon the cheeks,
Weeks,
Can pass
Until at last
Here comes the past
And it makes me blush
I'm already flushed
A giddy schoolgirl crush,
Like a little girl, unblemished and pure
Looking back I think that there's no cure
For innocence,
Since,
It can be given or taken away
And these thoughts do stray
From cotton white to scarlet red
I tread,
On dry land and soft spoken thoughts
Knowing I had caught
Up with an angel in the snow
And this angel does glow
And these feelings do grow
More and more,
What's in store...
Rose petals and candles scented
Bubble baths that seductively hinted
At deflowering a lily tinted
With a thought that tainted
This purity has painted
A beautiful scene
But what waits to be seen
...
Is it worth it

Does the actuality make you nervous
...Or scared...
These thoughts have cared
And caused a battle,
That'll
Do the damage
Damaged goods
Red roses could
Be a fitting synonym
Pain deep seated has wrought
Thoughts on a whim,
Emerging
Urging,
This virgin thought

They Say it's Complicated but I Think it's Simple

LoVe is... calculus in third grade,
home-made
German Chocolate cake from scratch
LoVe is... the match
Pyro keeps in his back pocket, it's the Tiffany locket
'round my neck,
chain too small
chokin' the life outta me LoVe
is... what I see
before I make choices, it's the voices ------- in my head
the lead
in the bullet, when u pull it (the trigger) to your head
left for dead,
Lead,
in pencil
traces our name in stencil, bubble letters with the heart,
it's the art, we keep barely passin' at
grades up to par
that writes do u like me
check yes or no
searchin' for that star
LoVe is... where we go
when the world gets too tough
it's the favorite auntie's hug, bff's smile
favorite lover's touch
it's always enough
To make everything okay
....startin' out.
but LoVe'll have u starin' out
into space
picturin' a face
that puts you in a spin
that day------------------ love turns u in
hands u a pink slip

then it's the master's whip
40 lashes cross your back
a backhanded pimp smack
with brass knuckles
LoVe can be ... that embarrassing uncle
at family reunions.
But then again LoVe is.....
the union
for better or worse.
It's the smile with one dimple
I thought LoVe was complicated but I get Him now
It's simple

*"End up a phone call away from those lonely winter days
When night hides secrets in a gin and tonic flask
The chronic illness of Bible clasped
Prayer hands that lack the grip to hold on to either
No longer pray
No longer prey but predator"*

II.

Silent cymbals, clashing

Void

So, trying to fill this void
A friend of mine toyed, with the notion of a boy
Friend, and found in this friend that tears end and cease to exist
A peace that persists...in unison
With the stringed quartet that reverberates in that heart
And the orchestra falls apart
When the lovemaking starts
...A state of constant dying begins
Then the pain ends...
The pain that sends velvet tears down her face'
puts in place Hurt
that place, a Heart
The Heart Hurt makes a trace of her heart in his hand
her tears in black sand
Then the tears end
...The tears that send traces of his fingertips down...
her spine...
her mind...is torn
A heart ... is worn
So trying to fill this void
A friend of mine toyed, with the notion of finding a completer
Someone or something that makes life sweeter
To the taste
In his face
... She could look through those windows and find an estimate of his soul
At that place
Where nothing even matters
She stepped up to bat with his matchless swagger
And got caught
And constantly sought
To hit the ball out the park
And strike a chord that could spark
An electrical fire
He's live wire

She's on fire...then the fire ends
The fire that sends
For reinforcements to put it out
After all, she put it out...there
And,
In a final attempt to fill this void
This same friend of mine employed
A healer to repair the damage
The damage starts from the inside out
She feels kinda overwhelmed, all burnt out.
Somewhat unworthy, not good enough,
Seldom happy, but often hot, sad, depressed, mad and stuff
Sinful, bad, full of lust
Physically attractive because she's thick enough...
Maybe too much
For some
But, um.....
She's confused because she didn't grow up in a fatherless home,
Had a stay-at-home mom so enough love was shown ... and attention given
So perfect it seems.
Feeling, so far from perfect she screams
But no noise
Such a perfect posture...but no poise
Consistent word flow...but no voice
Often lacking, she's annoyed...
Where did it come from, this void?
She's been thinkin' about fillin' the void for quite some time now
And despite him being often on her mind, somehow...
"Empty" doesn't go away because it stares back from the mirror
And as each day passes she sees clearer
She's scared that one day she really won't care
Because that same void will still be there
Meanwhile... I'm still tryin' to fill this void

Broken Rhyme

He's not brokenhearted
He's too broke to be guarded
Back to the Sun, skin darkened
Tracks in his lungs, sin hearkened
Wind sharpened, its blade and sometimes sucks the breath outta his soul. Fear soars
His arteries can't convince enough blood to flow through their passageways. Feel sores
I imagine he's a passerby lightning bolt caught in a cloud of acid rain
Classic pain
Perched on the tip of his tongue,
Like a clit and some cum,
We measure pulse, his wrist and his one
Heartbeat
From raw shit he has done
Listen, it's a full clip loaded gun
Full of sorrow, he manages to
Pull tomorrow
Out the discarded wrapper of what's protection
We put our trust in lust to borrow passion lasting longer than its erection
Caress the connection that holds love's neglect and dissects it
Just lets it, exist
Naked as this, poem
No discretion, necessary he tries not to sew 'em
Spills his seed on the earth
Thrills that heed to the birth
And I almost saw him cry, once
His back was turned but I saw his shoulders hunched
And shaking
At the daybreak, making him realize, he's human enough to hurt
Sees himself through real eyes that read between the lines of real lies
And dream of the ordinary

He's not brokenhearted
He's too broke to be guarded
He's got soul that needs a helmet like an epileptic retarded
Football player, he's got turpentine on his spine, glass sharded
And broke up
I imagine, he must've woke up, emotions paralyzed
When his twin brother was gone
Sometimes I look though those eyes, never cries, and hear a moan
I bet the grown, man in him is still holding out his hand for his brother
I tried to stitch up his chest
His heart beats outside his breast, for his mother
Sometimes he just needs compassion from another
Human being,
A week into our friendship, he confided
That the babysitter hided
Her womanhood in his pants
And his hands, had no matching mommy's to hold
No babysitter, but now
He got a baby girl, he sit her
On his lap, hoping he instinctively told, her everything she needs to know about this world
He needs to know, about this girl, all the gold
Ain't good enough
He shops at Abercrombie and wears smediums
He ain't hood enough,
But it's cool
I guess he's becoming full
Of himself
And in this world
Maybe that's all you really need
To keep your heart from being broken

Disney

Fairytales, in all their happily ever after glory
Should be buried in the closet with skeletons that hide the most perversely deviant stories...
But at least they're true.
And no, it's not picture perfect but the harshness of Love's struggles make her a better woman for the task.
Those pretenders should be remembered only as fake ash stories singed into the recesses of thousands of memories harassed by past
"Love" and the attached glory
Reality
The fatality of something unreal when it replaces and steals
....the attainable
The irony that it takes time to heal wounds inflicted by an illusory foe
...Friend
Once upon a time,
Way back when Belle found love among the embrace of a beast and learned his tender side
I tried
To duplicate, but faith in faith is a Beast
He's an undercover snitch with no swagger
Faith in fate led me to a ditch where I stagger
To stand
Stammer to exchange pleasantries and shake the hand
That shattered my glass slippers
A hand which with the remnants slit my wrists and dripped cursive writ L O V E in blood on snow. Sh...
Simplistic description of twisted sentiment that dares me to show...
Gratitude?
Currently my attitude
Shakespearean tragedies are more fitting metaphors
More synonymous with real life,
Two souls of opposite direction have met with a potentially fatal attraction and
Drank the concoction of a particularly potent potion

Sat in the contraption of a potentially fatal scheme, that begs and screams to be seen
For what it is
At this point, or so it seems, to mention Romeo and Juliet would be overkill, but still....
It's like Romeo and Juliet.

We Need

We walk hand in hand, with a flirty air
A subtle sexuality that starts to dare
Time to proceed.
We patiently wait for the hurrying of our birthdays
Constant indicators that we're a year closer to being older
Wantin' to be growner...
But we must admit, there are times when we long for a mother's touch
Something exists implicit in quivering lips
Her fingertips make treks and lay traces
Amidst the tears in our faces
Maybe the way her femininity graces
Our existence.
Traces of simplistic sadness saturate already sorrowful souls
And...
Not quite feeling whole
Unable to speak...

We kiss lip to cheek
Innocent sexuality,
Coupled with the reality
of us
Unsteadily,
Tongue-n-tongue
We plunge,
Headlong in a misguided direction
He kisses mouth to the lips of thighs wide open that learned what it means to assume the position.
He kisses... mouth to the lips of thighs wide open,
Assumes the position at a birth canal predestined to become a road to perdition
Damnation and salvation stationed our enmity on the basis of his and her seed
That being said,
There are times when
We need

A big sister's advice
The one who says... do you really want to lie on your back in a '94 Saturn...think twice.
Hot as ice

We stand, pelvis to hip, lips pursed, with lustful stares
Climbing stairs on all fours.
Ascending to new heights on old floors
Laced with antiquity and sordid care
A primitive sexuality that lays bare
Animalistic tendencies, intentions of a man driven by his head
A head
That desperately needs brain...Bent on riding our trains
Of thought to unheard of destinations
Explanations lie in
The close proximity of our openings.
The similarity of our desires
The mortality of our immorality
Thus femme fatale
Got caught in her familiarity of what boy and girl are made of
With boy in girl, our made love... Was semi-lethargic, not quite climactic
We won't admit to anyone else but...
There are times we need a big brother's protection
He who understands the simple complexity of the sex that falls prey to their own erection
No discretion...
Necessary.
Meanwhile
We smile,
Riding in cars with boys
'Till it's over,
When it's over

We walk, foot in mouth
Making it easier to stumble over words
And nearly impossible to walk away.
Not knowing how to look at him and say...

Daddy, I think I messed up.
I'm sorry.
Sometimes we need a father's sternness
But could do without his disappointed look
If you're a daddy's girl you discern this.
Over the years we earn this...
Right to walk down the path left of center.
We started out holding hands but in the end
Left a sinner.

Morning After

Peel,
Back the sheets like Elmer's glue off a hand 12 years prior
24 years of façade ridden liar, of a woman
The same messy kinda feeling
Thinly veiled and sanctity stealing senses
Since its'
Like weathering the Blizzard 2011 on Lake Shore Dr.
running out of gas.
And time….
Vision mine,
Eyes wide open shut
Now blistering cold gusts, through the windows to my soul and tucks my psyche in at night.
When at dusk returning light reminds me of that passionate struggle, the rumble
Some do,
Be basing life off of the fast track mentality
Let's back track…. And that'll be……..
…..eh-hem………….
Now blistering cold gusts rush through the windows to my soul,
Goooooaaaaaaallll!
Scored, soccer kicked, sucker punched
Leaving a draft and crimson touch, tide plunged nostalgia.
Disappointment ensues
Reminiscent tissues Kleenex the scene to clean ax the ex, freeze frame
New scene. Dream
Of a clearer image.
Talked off the ledge
Now sitting on the edge of the bed I see her in the mirror
Barely recognizable
Thighs buried what is hide-able
Though to most,
Those moans roast, over the open fire and never fully develop
Fully developed awareness, scares this woman

Such is the cognizance of the morning after.

The morning after
Peel
Back covers that covered nakedness, its stark contrasting beauty
To shame.
Though both are dark
The reality that sometimes the game, is just that
And find new ways to blame a nigga
A faceless figure with a trigger
You pull,
The shades open
Cascading waterfalls notice,
Murderous intent on a daily basis
Questionin' if it's even better to fuck familiar faces
Three bases, all skipped, end up at home
Debases, past judgment and end up alone
       End up a phone… Call away from those lonely winter days
When night hides secrets in a gin and tonic flask
The chronic illness of Bible clasped
Prayer hands that lack the grip to hold on to either
No longer pray
No longer prey but predator
The weatherer of snowflakes in a dimly lit synthesized room
Spoon fed the bass line to an old Chicago jazz club for a February doom….
Rather mood,
Mourning after
The morning after

Rebirth

He held my hand and led me down the road from saint to sinner
And if my subconscious realities are driven by sexuality
He delved into my crevices and became the winner
That brought a conscious finality
To the constant actuality that two people can stay hot even in winter
Let's say, if he learned all my spots, back to center
Or had a previous knowledge of them
We both know chances are slim
To none
Trying to escape unscathed...but I was that one
He chased,
Replaced...
When he was done,
Or realized we'd go no farther
Father,
Sometimes I feel, like I grew up overnight
At the age of 19 I went from 17 to 21 and it's like I had to fight,
All by myself,
And against myself
But I had friends in my corner
Yet and still I feel like I'm in a corner
Why did I have to be in the belly of the fish before my rebirth could begin?
Trying' to find the straight and narrow and follow it but around every corner lurks Sin
...He's drawin' me in
...Grabbin' my waist
...Holdin' my hand
...Lickin' his lips,
winkin' at me,
Sometimes I feel I'm the only one He sees
Thinkin' that he's, always in my peripheral
Symbolic but yet, quite literal
The purification of the mind starts with the heart

So if I take a teaspoon of sanctification maybe I'll bump into salvation and fall back in love with the art
Of being saintly
...Sometimes, I cain't be
I try, but it's like,
"Ain't he……………….sexy"
That one over there, I like his style
This one, I dig his aura
But when I look at that smile,
It's either Satan callin' me, or a…
Glimpse at heaven, in flesh and blood
Now there's a lot of leaven in my flesh and blood
Every so often I wish I could
Go back in time and change stuff
But I can't so I just hang tough
...and try and turn this sinner back to a saint
I guess it's something like a rebirth
…..so after this resurrection, I'll get up and wipe off the dirt,
Wipe off the hurt....
Of a saintly sinner

III

rhythmic love

"…Love is an art…
You try to capture a fistful of tears through an
expressive medium."

Brown Sugar

YOU are the perfect verse over a tight beat
I used to L.O.V.E. him
Love is a two way street
That I ride
To the rhythm of a bass line
And I cried
To the rhythm of a man, so fine
And I swayed
Back and forth amongst familiarity and circumstances, changed
And I weighed
The balance, finding my options not rearranged...
Just different
I'm different
He's different
This rhyme is so different
That it got me wonderin' if it's a love song
Each line is long
And filled with several words
That reminds me of something I heard...
Love without passion, can ironically breed lust
But adding stimulating conversation is the perfect touch
Plus
He has the perfect touch
I clutch
My breasts
Mind finds, little rest
Knowing the heart within this chest
Is beating so unsteadily
Rock steady, to the beat
The strings make us meet
Eye to eye
...Pelvis to hip...we stand
This man
Holds my hand
While trying to remember the title
Finger snappin'...break dancin'

Whoknows what/ may happen/...if we act on
our attraction... stancin', intimacy
Hip thrustin' contractions
Within Time standin' still, a fraction
Of life is lost to music's height
YOU are the perfect verse over a tight beat
You are Common's "The Light"

Convinced... Love

I was finally convinced that Love loved me
I'm not trying to make You be...
Unfaithful
But I'm grateful,
For You and me.
Honestly,
If I thought she deserved You I wouldn't be
As inviting
Truth is, I'm igniting what I've always tried to control
Truth is, you and I both know how to hold,
Each other just the right way
And a less than perfect day
Couldn't get any better
We both made up our minds that eventually we'd let Her...
in
Then
It began
And
If I could go back
I'm not sure I'd change anything
Despite the limited phone rings
The sting, of loneliness when you're not around
I feel like I've finally found, my footing
Float in mid-air while on solid ground
Ironically, it comes while I'm falling
Everyone knows You're who I'd be calling
If I ever needed a hand
And
I'd kiss it, 'cause I adore You
Did I tell You,
I think,
You're simply beautiful
One blink,
Dreams do come true.... I love You
Look at me,
Love,
I'm finally convinced that You love me

In His Image

Apologies in advance
But I think there's a chance
That from head to toe, this metaphor flows
Like Jesus' blood
Such beautiful blasphemy
    Floods
        My senses
My sentence, begins
His hair….. was like the wool, of sheep
His sentence begins with an earthly ministry, weeping
Teaching me how to love
An otherworldly chemistry
Attracts me to him
Gravity pulls me closer to his hands
His hands… seem to belong to the son of a carpenter
Inexperienced with a hammer
Imagine
I begin to stammer, when I notice nail holes
Accidental pale, froze
An impaled pose
And knees made weak, Bronze
Dusty feet from wearing sandals on Rainbow Beach, sweat
Musty heat's musk must await the tide to wash over the scandal
And betrayal, wet
Tears
Heartbroken poetry
Bloody hands,
Red as scarlet, washed white as snow
Whitewashed though
Looking at me through
The bluest eye ever.
Contacts…
Contract the vision of us through bodily contact
This imagery is clever
I envisioned me severed from his makeup
Formed from within him. One rib less.

Trying to break even
Just to be clear, we aren't Adam and Eve. This ain't Eden
I can't swim or fly, I just try to walk in the sand and not make new footprints
Now he can't perform miracles, but he held out his hand and I walked on water.
Did I mention, I can't swim
We write history into existence through our pens we author The Word
Sometimes, when the day seems grim, I notice a flicker of light
I might….
Be in need of salvation
But I think he just saved me.

Untold Story

A friend of mine challenged me to no longer let my love go untold
So I'll tell a story about this little girl, who, her heart she sold
To a boy who had a chest where he could keep and hold
...It safe and tight,
Until while lying in solitude in her bed one night
She couldn't sleep
She began to weep
Because these feelings do creep
Up out of nowhere
So, a prayer
Escaped from the confines of her soul
As she tearfully lamented that she was cold,
And wanted to be warm...
But she couldn't because her heart was gone and torn
Remember, she gave it to a boy
Don't mourn,
He did keep it safe just like he promised he would
But at the same time he held it so tight that she could
Never know just how much she was cherished
Until that day when the chest holding it perished
And became just a box with no key
It's already unlocked for all to see
She's bare
It's bold and naked
She can't take it,
Doesn't know how to make it
But never does she fake it
She just takes it
Back
To her memories
When he was the centerpiece
Of this now fatal attraction,
If every heart held pain like contractions
She would hold in her womb
Life instead of doom

And give birth to a brand new tomorrow
Then she'd grasp for air while throwing sorrow
Away
Just pray
That he gives her heart back and soon...and when...
She needs to be warm again...
She'll know she was never cold in the first place
I bet she still remembers his face
I bet she'll remember every trace...
He made around her heart
What if this girl can't start,
To remember, but wants to forget
See, she has difficulty expressing verbally
How she's feeling inside
What if she's scared because everytime she opened that box or gave away the key it cried
And cried
And cried
I tried
To tell her not so perfect story clearly
What if I can't tell the story right because the untold story mirrors me

Imperfect Conversation

Hey you...
your imperfections make you beautiful
did you know,
I value your flaws
Now let's just apply the laws
Of gravity
U have to be
Heavenly
'Cause when you walk your feet don't touch the ground
And I don't mean to sound
...Repetitive...
But, your imperfections make you beautiful
I mean it too
By the way, I've been meaning to ask you
Why do you look down when you smile?
I'll,
Speak nothing less than the honest truth when I say you have the most beautiful smile I have ever seen
Not trying to be mean...
To others
But no mother, father, sister, or brother's
Smile comes close to yours
Meaning it was created especially for you
And it's true...
You
Turn heads and open doors
With your intelligence
Now, you're no genius
but
Your imperfections make you beautiful
I was wonderin' if when the wind blew
You hear it calling your name
telling you, "April, have no shame...
For life's a game
And you're your own player"
Now let's offer up a prayer
For your imperfections

Because you're imperfect
Yet and still a beauty
Truly,
Let's sing...
Some India.Arie
Let's heal the disconnection
Become purified and grab hold of sanctification
For yourself
...By the way
I like the way your eyes shine
When you laugh
When you're happy
When you look at peace
And sometimes I find
peace
Of mind
With your originality
And individuality
Expressively expressing what it means to be me
What it means to be free
Be yourself
...Who needs wealth
When your imperfections make you beautiful
And cause sensations
That may or may not go unnoticed by others
But that doesn't really matter anyway
Because you have no mistakes
Just systematic imperfections
So while lookin' in the mirror
You see a lil' bit clearer
The divinity of your beauty
And infinity of yours truly
In recognizing,
No disguising...
Through this imperfect conversation with self, ... that
Your imperfections make you beautiful

Pronoun's Love

"Us" starts with you, ends with "s", possibly for indiscretions so often swept
Under the rug where we slept, corners creek where we crept,
Warmth of the summer night where we... took a leap of faith
Of love,
Leapt off the ledge, pushed to the edge
Of climactic stimulation
Ultimately elevation, of senses
There are uncertain suspenses, concerning what the future will bring
Maybe the sting, of loneliness
Maybe it won't last forever.
Maybe...

We started with palms upward, both hands opened, awoke then, within desires...
Thin skin makes one feel every sensation, the fires,
The fine fibers wire, us
When dwellin' within' the warm, wet, waterfalls of familiarity
This familiar phase displays the similarity with which we lay and lays
Today and days...before ------------ yesterday, the other day and way into the future
The future, used ta look a little different
Did I mention,

"We" starts with a double you, ends with an "e", possibly for everything we put into intimacy
The inclimate-cy of the weather makes the storm of us difficult to bear
I wear, tornado torn remnants of sleeves
Slipped through the slashes and dashes, stashes of slits, guiltless make believe
Guileless retrieve-------al of your heart, our art..........

Stashed as the centerpiece
Emotionless tears, lay motionless... frozen heat... where I grieve
-----And cuffs are numb to it
Your touch, I succumb to it.
Bob and weave to avoid the throb and sting of punches to the gut, just reprieve.
A standstill strut, to adjust my stance
Stuck in a rut of mucked up
Circumstance-------------ces
Perhaps our happening to be here happens to be happenstance--------------ces
Over and over, again
We hold each other's heart in hand
And slow dance to hip hop swappin' quick chances at romance. Occasionally
Steals glances at the hour
At hand,
At hand, So many hours dedicated to our heart. Minute minutes met absentmindedly meditating on the meditations of my heart.
Namely "you"
Medication is no healer
Ask the reflection, "Can you hear her?"
Muted speech beseeches methods to preach and teaches deaf listeners how to pronounce love
Pronoun's love
At the hour
At hand --------- At hand

"Our" begins with oxygen, ends with rest and has you in between,
That means,
Each breath is consumed by us
We occupy every waking hour and sleeping dream, plus
It seems,
Our inner rhythms are finely defined arithmetic
But I can't calculate how to get us.
All I know is
I get us.

I love u.

School Subjects

I was always better at English than Math
Maybe I should've kept it that way
That way,
I could've written all the love poems and songs about love and happiness and making us stay
Together,
Together I thought we were simple addition
$1+1=2$
But you,
Are a complicated melody and the most beautiful rendition
Of an algebraic expression,
The combination of numbers and letters
And I get wetter
Than science should allow...
But back to math, and now
I know
I always tried to be the one constant in your life
Making it impossible to find the solution without me
I was attempting to add up all the variables and still equal us
Steal us equal planes and trains of thought
But I fought
With paper and pen in hand
...Can't do the math, my pencil's lead broke and it has no eraser
But I can write you a poem or story,
It begins,
"Have you ever tried to face her..."
But the mirror's distorted.
I sorted
Out my closet and found history
In the pattern's mystery
In the old cloth's misery
...In the cognizance of our familiarity with what lies beneath the fabric
When on us...
Him on us,

Skin on us,
Then the rush of lust
Sin on us,
Then the rust of us,
I guess history gets old
Have I told, you that I thought we were writing history as each day passed
Didn't you tell me what's done is done, you can't change the past
But run with it...
So I run with it
We ran with it
U sit down and then stand in it, rather....
What we were, everytime our eyes meet...
All this running sounds like a track meet, but I was never on a team
And there's no "I" in team but it is in win so I guess you won my heart
Now here comes the hard part
... Love is an art...
You try to capture a fistful of tears through an expressive medium
And I admit, I go insane, crazy sometimes, trying to keep you from losing your mind...
But in time, I find that what's mine is mine but I'd sign over the deed to my heart and mind
So you can keep it safe
It's already yours why not finish the paperwork and then lock it in a safe?
Make it official
I graduated from school but I'm still learning you, true
You're English, we're Math and in the process of making History
It's official...
But I'm not through
Yet...

Class in Session

In biology class,
I sit at my desk nervously looking over my shoulder
In every nook and cranny, corner and crevice
I keep looking for a spider
Gargantuan,
Your skin really does feel like silk. You must hide her
In the web where you hide me
I hope she's not envious because you confide in me
You must've had 20/20 vision to find me
    And paid attention to every intricate detail...
Before I had GPS installed to find myself
An internal compass,
Now we sit like a collection of Langston Hughes poetry on a Harold Washington Library 2nd floor shelf
And descend crystal stairs together
Hand in hand
We fit together like thousands of tiny grains of sand
On the shore of Lake Michigan, with no breeze
With so much ease, they lay
They allow the lake to steal all the glory and don't utter a sound
Just when I think I can't find the ground
You catch me
I got the matching latch key for the deadbolt lock on that safe
In the center of your chest
Feel safe. We're the only two sinners left, in this perfect world
My favorite sense is touch because I feel you so well, despite the twirl of the Earth spinnin' off its axis
Ask this: Do u feel like you could be stuck in 6 x 8 ft. cell
With me? Sometimes when we're holding hands I feel the DNA in our cells
Our fingers intertwined like an infinite labyrinth of desire, love spells...
The lines in our palms have just enough time to discover their interconnectedness

Lying in your arms, I felt a nakedness
In the universe
That was first experienced in Eden after indulging in fruit
Are you the curse
That gave me my first taste of a bittersweet romance
With blindfolds on we jump at the chance to dance, to our own tune.
Roses in full bloom with thorns blurting out warnings.
Cassettes in tape decks with beats that spurt out bass less recordings
Of lust.
Plus, the boom box has a busted speaker.
So, we make our own music. Become our own teachers
Learn, that we should thank earthly and celestial bodies
I whisper my secret
      He fell
      From the stars so I pluck and clip wings weekly
I love the emphasis you place on detail…
We tell,
      Our story in braille
      My body the template for everything hidden, bed ridden sincerity
      Clarity,
With charcoal and pencils you draw up the sketch,
Blindly
We sneak peeks at blood spatters and love notes scattered
And all sixteen fingertips follow the patterns we etch

Poem Speak

Yeah,
Okay,
Let's just say... I shouldn't say, this.
I shouldn't admit what I miss
Most
But words don't come close
And writing does it no justice
Just this...One poem
Has to make u feel it
Make u understand
And that emotion, reel it
Back to my heart through both hands
...Clasped tightly
I might be
Trying' to write, so I can see
Pass the past
When first kisses became last
Wishes
That we both misses
I'm not Mrs. ...yet
But his remembrance alone gets me...
WAIT
I'm trying to forget
Really I am
Don't want to think about endless possibilities
Of how things would be if he made love to me
...Just the way I wanted it
And we both know I wanted it
And we both know he wanted it
And after knowing what you want it's hard to move on
...For me at least
Feeling like, the intimacy we share makes me grown
But honestly
Only grown folk should be intimate
...If that's the truth...
I can be no youth
For he evoked adult feelings

Now before I start healing
I need to feel like I am better off without him...
So do I?
Even still, I'm not quite sure...
Who needs friendship
When there can be romance
When there can be no chance
Of platonic relationships
If you get what this poem is hintin' at
Let me know what I'm getting' at
Because sometimes I feel
As though my emotions spill
Through the ink
Meanwhile I think...
Thoughtlessly
His caresses be
Mentally
Hindering
Me...
On the subconscious level
Searching for a large black shovel
To bury what was had
Lost and found
Triggering clamorous silence all around
Maybe that's this poem doing all the talking
Maybe that's this pen independently walking
All over the page...
To create a stage...
of just,
..........."Poem Speak"

IV.

bass blaring headphones, screaming lyrics, failing organs, crying violins, Treble Heartbreak

---

"I play the games that kids play, you speak the words that tears pray...when gravity pulls them heavenward. Hot air balloon love, it's combustible."

Five Reasons for Apologies

One,
I play the games that kids play
You speak the words that tears pray
When gravity pulls them heavenward
    Hot air balloon love, it's combustible.
Two,
Today my voice sounded like helium and a pin prick
We've been together through thin thick situations
And I get the fact that sometimes negations overshadow the bright plusses
Today, your voice sounded like it was choking on our memories
I put all my energies into CPR, but it's impossible to revive our future
You told me nothing can change it
I guess there's no sense in me trying to rearrange it.
Three,
Fifty-seven times I hit redial
I was ignored about thirty, and when you finally pick up
I have four minutes and less than two hundred fifty characters to transport my heart from my chest to the tip of my tongue.
It had a hard time breaking out its cage
Ribbed t-shirt rage with more lines to remind me that I'm running out of space and time
Lately our conversations remind me of running with a wrist full of bangles in a quiet room
Our mistakes dangle like wistful femininity on the Lake front during July noon
Silence ensues at the most awkward moment. I'm noisy
And it's too hot to be too girly, swirly
Overly emotional.
This ain't cute.
Four,
How long does it take to
Put your regrets in a suitcase and board a flight to the future

Without your best friend.
I'm hoping I can catch it when, I sneak in the overhead compartment
I'll make the reservations... Take Southwest
Bags fly free,
And we got a lot of luggage
A few carry-ons
A terminal full of yesterdays
How can you run away from me on the runway where we hover over the present?
Presently, my mind jogging in place.
Five,
If I could, I would retrace our steps to that March and then hopscotch over them to this early May day.
Back then we were too busy being each other's Saviors to hear the echoes
    Mayday................. Mayday
We may say, we make mistakes and now it shakes the very foundation of our relationship
Make day brighter at day break by acknowledging we make stakes higher and then bet on them as if our very survival depends on it
And it does
So let me trace your outline in pencil and then erase the mental lapses
I apologize I never meant to be the sentimental collapses
Of everything right with us.
Just watch this
You say a year from now we'll look back and laugh
I hope so
I'm running a little behind schedule
And you're sitting waiting.
We're like synchronized watches
And they keep on debating
    On whose got the timing right
I no longer care about rhyming right,
I just want you to accept what I write.
    And know my apology took the form of a poem
        because sometimes the words don't
come out..... the way I want them to.

Letting Go Of Safe

my right hand grabbed my left wrist
and wouldn't let go
even that didn't work, my fingers still reach for your throat
trying to hold on to our breath
literally

I want you to always remember me.
Remember me?

trying to let go, half-heartedly though
you got a crazy glue palm print on my heart
an outlined hand indented in my chest like clay
a right wrist handcuffed to my long term memory
... I keep forgetting how not to remember what you say,
and how you used to say it...
feet shackled to my temple,
every step you take walking away from me, I get
migraines. I can't take it...
Honestly,
I keep you safe in a shoebox under my bed like poems and
love letters ten years young
handwritten notes,
your penmanship bleeds apologies like the beginning of
puberty
tears flow like the heavy flood of first days and last kisses
we end with the same finality of its punctuation. Period.
the start,
uncertain and embarrassed
still searching for the careless
caress that rested crested in your chest, ignoring the
murmurs, trying to find its beat again

I don't know if the wind, of today's tornado warning, knew
the world was supposed to end,
yesterday...
yesterday, you called me
I realize, my phone doesn't have a tone that fits you

but I know even it miss you
I keep you
in my back pocket, like the only safe card I've ever known
I've never owned
enough courage to be totally myself, but I know about that shelf
where my pride sits like an MVP trophy I've never won
aging, getting older

so, is this the ton
of really letting go that's sitting upright on my shoulders

These Days Lately

And on that day
About 2 weeks ago,
I watched you close the door behind you and board the Metra back to Chicago
It felt like the end
I felt my heart bend
And twist and jump and shake
I thought it would break
But it didn't
It just melted
Came oozing out my pores
Left bruising and a sore on my left chest
About 8 cracked ribs and a tender breast
I attempt to rest
But can't

And on that day
About a week ago
I sat on the couch in my 1 bedroom apartment and realized that within the 4 corners of every room at least 4 things remind me of you
Sadness hangs on each wall with a familiarly odd sentiment
That your living portrait went...
And the echo of your booming voice and boisterous laugh doesn't stick around nowadays
Now in no way, am I a mathematician
But I can't seem to divide us and still equal me... whole
On my own.
Its funny how being grown, makes me wish I were a kid again
I'm playing hide and seek with men, I barely even know
Wish I could hide when I told you everything there is to know
About me
Sometimes I doubt me
Sometimes my skin seems too thin to secure all my insecurities

You're to me
The purity,
That vanishes with loss virginity
I attempt to remember me
But can't.

And yesterday
About 24 hours ago
I'm reminded of our song.
I lie on my bed, facing the window, my back to the two doors and one mirror in between.
I hear bones.
Crashing and falling, tumbling over hangers, shoes,
Rubbermaid storage bins and the Macy's comforter set you gave me
So is this the new brave me
Or maybe there's a grave
We buried all the grotesqueness in
Mainly just our battered, betrayed hearts or the remaining remnant. Our sin
Our secrets. The admittance of shames and guilt, atrocities of character, neurotic tendencies
We barricade our hurt in the panic room of a Southside tenement
Really, I want to clean out my closet
But honest.
...I have nowhere to put all these skeletons.

Love DeLorean

You'll call in fifteen days and say let's go back to the future
I hate to say I told you so, but remember you used ta....
Remind me what we're doing this for
Never mind.
Just before you close that door
Let's make love on the floor, I'll adjust the TV so it's watching you
Muted
Breathing never sounded so heavy,
Breathing heavily never seemed so effortless
Fingertips never knew they could dance as though they were a pianist's lover and we keep turning to black and white
Vintage channels
Black and white keys
Track the light, seas seem to cease their flow
I know,
That cracked hourglass' sand is steadily spilling through, taunting us
    The sounds you make at the moment haunting, must everyone know our little secret
I'll set the DVR to record so everytime you play back your favorite show you can hear my heart breaking
Listen closely, can you hear my ribcage shaking
Five heartbeats taking the bassline by the throat, making my breathing shallow
Does It sound more like Motown or neo soul?
You hold,
Me tight, whisper don't let go
I Lego my pride and let the building blocks topple to the floor
That same floor, reminds me
Of carpet burned skin...so soft
The artic yearned wind, fire and ice tossed
In the balance
When the balance

Was lost and we couldn't get our positioning just right...
Let's edit the VHS
Rearrange how we see sex mess
Play in slow motion and call it love creating
Fast forward and the rename I'm debating, don't call it fucking
Call it the lust imploring love destroying marriage of passion and privates
I know we got a 1987 vinyl album full of Pandora regrets
Let's let the scratches press the reset
Button and the needle skip over the present
Our history is beautiful, never ending but it's always pouring in to right now
What about tomorrow
Will you love me come summer, 'cause I'm a spring kinda girl, in autumn I always fall
And I miss the winter
That's when the series started and I can't catch the episodes on demand
In about fifteen days, you'll tell me lets go back to the future
And This,
Will be the last time

Guilt and Tears

Please excuse the tears in my eyes
Thumbs on my trachea,
Fingertips on the nape of my neck

It's not that I'm crying again
Just right now, all choked up trying to mend
Stitch up the skin where my lungs where ripped out
Tying our sin to a black laced corset where love skipped out
The back door
I woke up wondering if I'm dying, wind
Cradling me like a newborn baby
Skin possesses just enough melanin to convince itself
That if black is beautiful being brown is divinity to the 3rd power times crazy
And within this ancient colored girl complex
A dilemma divine is not knowing if I need a man to validate my triumphs.
Three hundred sixty five days of dry humps and lost love later
I sit in the crater of my own insecurity and longing, reflecting
I thought I was just letting
Go,
I think I should let you know, it's not your fault
Halt...
You used to say I was like your sister.
I guess that makes what we did incest
Unless the incense burning didn't smell like sex
It incensed the yearning beating in the middle of our chests
Like snare drums, the sounds in the headphones became so loud
I used to forget if I was in mid-air or the ground when the pound of your love came smashing in like a sledge hammer
I used a wedge to open that tight space and get out my grammar
Just right
Lips sealed tight

I just might, love you perfectly for the rest of your life
I stammer, I know I meant every word
And I'm sorry if our friendship is in jeopardy
But trivial pursuit games give me a full arsenal of weaponry
To convince you why you should just pick that category
Drop the stigmas, ignore what they say, you and I both know the gray
Area is always where our angles collided
No lie, I confided in your conscience
I fell in love with you so hard I was left unconscious
And dazed
I apologize, but days
Spent as a recluse have left me remembering the wreck you
Saw and saved, picked up and shaped
Into the woman I am now
Somehow,
We manage to keep our fingers and toes crossed just when we question
The probability of survival
No doubt,
Ever.
Never
Wonder
And if I ever have a daughter, she'll be my redemption song that I wake up and fall asleep to on a 12 hour interim
You're the whim of good grace that comes around once in a lifetime
This life's mine
In life my mind
Never knew a beauty so divine
It made me wanna stop breathing and steal all the air
Hide it somewhere, away from all the pollution and harness it. I'd dare
You to say you wanna breathe without me
We got guilty tears that best friends sometimes share
…But don't you just love everything about me…

Losing Religion

Idolatrous,
How you put me on a pedestal
Embezzlement,
Love, laughter, smiles, quick kiss, slick Ms., lick this, trick missed, feeling this
Unworthy,
Make me believe I'm special
Play make believe, let's take the sexual
Non-refundable, non-regrettable...
I ain't god, but I bet I can make you stay lest you
Forget to remember the mother
Marry
Me,
Bless you,
I'll let you
Crayola-color the sky red orange.
Our exploding hearts...
Imploding art of touch and senses
Praying for menses within the cycle of sins its'
The rebirth of sinnin'
In the beginnin' god created the heavens and earth
You created seven days of worth
And I, heart beating outside its chest, cracked ribs, tears froze
You, placed the Pacific Ocean at my toes
Told me,
Find the beauty in my reflection I'm worthy
    Showed me
How to walk on water
Now I author
The autobiographical script of us, like a recipe for your favorite unnatural disaster – at its climax
High calories, bake me my favorite dish – relax
Allergies make me sneeze, blasphemy and ish
And yet
You dare to love at my throne
Once more

Roam into the zone where the devilish girl seeks to devour.
    I defy you,
Christ
    Three times I denied you
Love...
    I'm sorry
    Repent and pray, incessantly
    We speak and say, its lessons we
    Learn as we grow in life, hesitantly
    Letting go of safe
Love...
    I'm sorry
    High stakes, bets placed on mistakes lets me play
Russian Roulettes
    Stand with the pose of brokenhearted silhouettes
shadow boxing their regrets
    I want a Novocain shot to the neck, head
    To numb the pain of our memories, lead to the brain
    Last December we
    Stood honestly, naked in front of a sea of faceless
faces and looked the serpent in the eye
    Never ever wanted to be so close and far apart at
exactly the same time
    Game mine, shame mine, tamed mind frame of mind
    Limbless, palms sweaty
    I wish I could hold you with an open mind and
closing arms
    Let me
    Go back and find
    My clothes on the Mars of your Milky Way
    Go back to that silky day and find
    What you saw in me
    Never meant to stairway to heaven climb with my
left heel on your spine
    Dug in with my toes
I should've told you those
    Dreams are dreams for a reason
    We wear pain like heartbreak is in season
    But those tears be seizin' my soul
Open exposed.

      You can only take so much
      Crystal can only break so much
      Bedtime stories make daybreak so much, brighter
      Eden, so much lighter
That fruit, I'm a biter
Idolatrous,
      How I offer you some

If Only You Knew

This morning, my spirit refused to answer the wakeup call
It just wouldn't roll over,
My body, still got out of bed
Leaving salt on my left shoulder
If only to cry the child in me back to sleep. This lead
In my heart, brain dead with depression
Lord let's let the leaven lessen
Let the subtle aggression, of having nothing to live for motivate us to exist
Let's reminisce
I need you to believe the innocence in me never meant to abandon the one constant in my life
In a sense I'm guilty
In this, my life
Is far from perfect
This life sentence doesn't fit
I admit I prefer it.
death
Yesterday, I couldn't find enough painkillers to numb my soul
So I learned hurt,
In its rawest form... dirt screaming for my burial
The soil could wash over me
There is something absolutely devastating
In the finality of your tone
This groan
In my gut,
What
Am I to do?
This full grown moan in my bones
My ribs ache... Let's take
Back the test I failed
Let's say, I put you on a godlike pedestal
And hailed, you as the firstborn of all creation
My mistake was making
Promises I could never keep

Days like this, those secrets seep through slightly parted pursed lips
Those bones, grim reaped, keep the closet door from closing
They keep falling
These voices keep screamin'
We all got demons, Jesus
Hasn't given us the authority to expel
These passions tend to dwell in secret places
We search for the moment when heart speak traces
Of friendship, gift wrapped regret
We can't let the words escape from our throat
Let alone roll off our tongue
Sensitivity fought way too hard to become numb
Now
They reside in the dark, damp sanctuary
That beating drum,
Ain't it scary...
When the gods kick you out of heaven
All this leaven
In imperfect love.
Last night, I couldn't dial 911 quick enough
I felt a two handed, grown ass man stab to the chest, a six inch deep
Wound. Still bleeding
Still can't speak
Still make believing your forgiveness will let me sleep
Honest, I've spent the past thirty-six hours learning how to breathe without you
Still gasping for air
And I keep inhaling, waiting for a call or text with you there
Yet to exhale
Swear
It hurts, knowing how much I care
And I now know how much I failed, and I dared
Our love to last, gambled it away for cheap liquor
This bruised heart induced hangover won't even put you in the right picture
So I put in a right handed pitcher and gave it my best swing.

But you left, just walked right off the field.
And I can't blame you
Simultaneously learning methods that inevitably maim you.
I've spent the past five years of my life putting everything into loving you right. The way you deserve
I guess I have a funny way of showing it.
I guess I feel in my tummy I know it, you knew it.
I've spent eight years perfecting the art of procrastination
Lesson learned: never treat love like high school or college work
I wait to the last minute. I'm always gone do it.
It just never eventuates
Well eventually
Essentially,
I took your love for granted
How do you tell the reflection in the mirror that the whole heart you planted,
Wasn't a suitable match for the donor all along?
You put every organ into loving someone and they tell you, you did it all wrong
And I keep playing the radio
And I keep hearing songs, that remind me of everything right with our relationship
While the music reminds me of what's wrong
So yesterday,
I was fighting back tears until I turned down Greenleaf and Patti Labelle came on
Your song...
Never fit so perfectly
You always said, there's a song for every occasion
She was crying too, that note had all types of abrasions
That matched the scarring on my heart
Things in my life start to fall apart. I've always expected you to piece them back together
Unfairly, found solace in the hands of a super glue hero who stayed dry no matter the weather
Whether right or wrong, depended on you for support so long I forgot how to bend
Never had the audacity to stand up anything but straight but forced you horizontal

Now it's the end
Now we're broke and I don't have the words to mend us
So I'll send an accident report to the universe
Maybe the stars can lend us
Just enough light to see past this.
Just enough song to sing past this.
Because…
I must have rehearsed my lines
A thousand times
Until I had them memorized
But when I get up the nerve
To tell you, the words
Just never seem to come out right

V.

7 day weather forecast – rain tapped percussion

> "Honestly, I think thunderstorms come to disrupt the sunrise.
> Is there any surprise that sometimes,
> The sun tries,
> To ignore the fact that you're beautifully human?
> At the end of the day, I can't forget
> I see your reflection in every cloud and puddle."

Sunrise

Sometimes
Sun tries
Not to shine so brightly,
She might be
    Knowing there's no competition...
Sunrise?
    Or was that my imperfections peaking at you
    Speaking the truth
    My faults find honesty sneaking to the youth
Of first kisses
Blisses, solar eclipses, me one day being your misses
                      Your smile, somewhere
Lost on the horizon
Searching Lake Michigan for those secrets, love's disguisin'
...we buried 'em in each other like hidden treasures
Now the sand meets the water with a sure measure
Of profound resentment
    The sound,
        Resounding discontentment
        Waves pounding at the sentiment
Of long walks on the beach
Listening to your heart preach, murmur and whisper that
I'm your heart and will always be
You gotta know, I gave you the best of me
No questions asked
    You're my pulse
    Together, we're the last
        Heartbeat of a dying love
We journey to where the dark meets blue sky
Our differences contrast like night and day
We fight and say
Let's make up forever
There are times when infinity stops at never
Just to remind Him, of sunrise
That sometimes
The sun tries
Not to shine too brightly

She might be
Wondering if she's worth saving
For a rainy day
The drainy gray of the 8am thunderstorm, was preceded only by the norm
Of the sun briefly peaking at you...
Who knew, cumulus clouds would hide her from you
How come you,
    No longer play in the rain?
      I remember the hunger, the pain
                  Of uncertainty

I'm hurtin', we
Were supposed to last forever
             Like the sun
It's burning,
I'm yearning
Do you understand how discerning
    What would be best ultimately broke us up
The lightning broke up
    The serenity of the sky
The thunder sounded like the first time you and I
                            Made love
And I wonder, if this sensation is really you within the rain,
    Making we wet...   with tears
Vision blurred...
    It's suddenly difficult to peer
At my future without seeing you in it
    And to think, you already knew, before the weather started sinnin'
                That this, was comin'

Honestly, I think thunderstorms come to disrupt the sunrise
Is there any surprise that sometimes
The sun tries
To ignore the fact that you're beautifully human
At the end of the day, I can't forget
I see your reflection in every cloud and puddle
I'm sitting on stars,
              Waiting for the sunset

                        One step closer to dawn
                        A heartbeat nearer to morning
No more mourning,
Just you
Sunrise

March Madness

In transition,
I got a crossover, hop step, dribble penetration move
You, go for the pull up open three
I'm hoping we
Aren't a one and done
Kinda team
I know we play a run and gun style offense
But they keep getting open looks at the basket, I sometimes mean
To let you in my bracket,
But that letting people in my space thing… I lack it
3 ft. no pressure…
Sometimes it's like we're playing 21 in the backyard where telephone lines and cracked concrete
Force us to measure our skills differently
I meant it we
Gotta adjust to the physical landscape because interference can't be called on stationary objects.
And yes, it may seem like it, but our hearts aren't taking charges
And yes, those stairs were always there. Stop making barges,
Don't fall.
I hate it when the refs make bad calls, to bail out the star
You fell out the star,
It was burning, I saw the permanent marks on your back. Was the pavement on fire?
That must be where you got your hops from. You always did have a knack
For being in position
Did I mention
This tourney madness got me on a journey
To VCU you
Sorry, I don't really want to upset you
This game is just so full of upsets
You con, me out of my heart and its precious jewels
You did say

You prefer those diamonds that claim the America's favorite pastime hold
To that squeak of Jordans on hardwood floors
Classics,
Diving catches and home runs
Over half-court buzzer beaters and alley oops
Sitting on tops of roofs, to watch the Cubbies at Wrigley Field
Over standing in line in the dead of winter, on Madison to get into the United Center
Web gems over dunks of the night
I know sooner or later, we might fight
About it
But I can't doubt it
We got a Jimmer range long distance shot at making it
And he made those, consistently
At least we both can agree on one thing
Just listen to me, no glass slippers to break,
No worry
My kicks laced up and double knotted fit perfectly
We might just be a Cinderella story

A...Typical Storm

Through the storm... Rain
Steadily hits the window pane, the window pain
Makes for easy observation of hurt... plus the stain
Of loneliness
If only this, weren't everlasting
Constantly contrasting emotions
The inward commotions --- unceasing
The rain,
Unceasing
As releasing tears flow heavy, fears learn to go steady
In uncommitted relationships with hurt
Trampled dirt plus rain equals mud -------- stained
Surfaces
Nervousness during storms makes me reminiscent of warm weather
Whether or not vacations learned to let her, be
Wetter, and an anatomy ill fitted for tropics
Searching for topics
Of discussion
That won't lead to concussions and headaches, back aches from dead weight ------- current repercussions
In the background, a symphony or rain tapped percussion
Instruments
Intimate imaginings of that special percussion
Musical f---ing
Rather lovemaking
Through the storm... Lightning
Reminds me of Greek gods ancient mythologies
Consummation is creation, Adam and Eve theology
Probably
Torrential downpour offset the disconnect of woman and man
She and he saw the serpent
And earth went
Into a familiar zone, unfamiliar to us
Lightning
Quick!

The rush
Comes quickly, but lasts forever
Intermingled with the blood and sweat
The rib severed
From him
Grim
Reaper.........
Through the storm ... Thunder
Sounds down
Blurts out warnings "Don't keep her!"
Thunder sounds indicate theistic indignation
Perception
Affected by loss visibility
Senses strained... blood drained
Through rough terrain
And rugged conditions
Premonition
Of tornado torn remnants of sleeves, where I grieve
Driving
Through the storm...
Then the swarm...
Of emotions
After the storm... Rainbow
Then the pain go
From the heart out
We often start out
Knees bent, prostrate, hands clasped tightly
Looking heavenward
I might be
Searching for sunny skies again
Seeking shelter from the cold
They say at the end of the storm
-- there's a rainbow
Where's my pot of gold?

MUSIC

Music is pure
It's kinda like true love...
It connects in a way
That makes us wanna fall in love
In my mind I'm hearing songs
I actually heard an hour ago
And sometimes I still feel him
But I last saw him a while ago
Music is pure
It's kinda like true love...
The pulsating rhythms
Are like my unsteady heartbeats
And the louder the bass
The louder my heart beats
As the chorus is sung
I'm carried away
When the voices are heard
All else, seems to drift away
When I stand up to dance
I'm in an unfamiliar place
But when he takes my hand
All else, falls into place
Music is pure
It's kinda like true love...
Like the air I breathe
It's sustaining me
Like the writing of poetry
It becomes a part of me
Music is...
      Melodies so melodic
           They tickle my ear
                 Harmonies so exotic
                      I wanna pull him near
Emotions are stirred up
Before words are even spoken
The sensation of even thinkin'
"Later he might be the one on one knee proposin"

Music has the harmonious chords intertwined just right
Just like our cardiac and intellect intertwined at first sight

Music is pure
It's kinda like true love...

Soulmate/Stormy Weather

My Soulmate and I
Haven't been getting along
Lately,
We can't seem to agree
On anything,
Not even a specific song
I've come to realize "why?"
We're searching for different things
Headed down different paths
 "How can we see eye to eye?"
    It's sad
      We had something special
      More or less   REAL
Huddled
Close knit
To keep each other warm
On cold windy days
In this cold Windy City
Now I got Inner City Blues
And only the Blues
    Are a reliable remedy
      Inwardly
I'm seeking what was so commonly unCommon
...Sense...
Since a concoction of the sort
Like Chocolate for Water
      Makes the hurt
  Easier to swallow
  Less likely to resurface
  I too appear calm though nervous,
My feelings SHOUT out...
In brief spurts
Utterances silent enough
Those Mos Def individuals can learn
What it sounds like
When Doves Cry
Those Mos Def individuals can hear

Of a town in Chyna Black
That clothed Charlene and Lucille
And fed 'em Cornbread, Fish and Collard Greens
So Anthony Hamilton could sing about that
"Soulmate, if ya listening..."
    Take note
    Brown sugar
    Brown skin
    Lost lover
    Found when
    Caught hunger
    Bound sin
        In
                The Truth and A Beautiful Surprise
...Otherwise...
        Nothing Even Matters
...Unless...
Linked to my naked Soul
   Child cries are caught in
     My innocent venom
        Sought after my sinister pride
             Before slaughtering emotions that coincide
                     With
My soulmate and I
        I
Don't even know if there's a cure
But "Hey You"
    WhoKnows,
    Dontchange,
    Love...
            Always finds a way
            If that's what you call it
            All it
             Does is
              Questions
            This   connection
                    Affection unparalleled
"Have we met before?"
     I think Musiq got me caught up
              ...but...

                What for...
We've been dating through centuries
You got me through miseries
And provided the chemistry
        To make it go away
                    And cease
        Pain and everyday
                    The peace
        You brought
                    Everlasting
                    The clashing
                    Of cultures
To produce Jay Linkin' Park-Z
Makes melodies matrimony an intrinsic part of me
                    Hypnotically attached
                    Fanatically attacks
            The well being
        Brings energy to the Max
Well, I'm Fortunate for my soulmate
            And just knowing
            Then seeing
            Who be fly
                And only
                Agreeing
                On Fu-gee-la
'Cause I'm pourin' beads of sweat
Into a cup of malice
And Lauryn, Pras, Wycl...
Rather, Lauryn's prize
Was possessing the rarest, talent
                            Alive

And I tried
To stay Black on Both Sides
But I cried
And I ...know not why
Maybe
            It's this Beautiful Struggle
            That makes Still
            Matics deprive deprivation
            And kill an unborn nation

But,
        All I know is
        I lost my soulmate
        And we gotta get back together
        'Cause I love music
            We date
        But we're approaching stormy weather

Abstract Complexity

And now,
I cry
Lying in the brevity
Of our inhalations
One deep breath
Exhales with the complexity
Of our intermingling,
Two bodies
Consciously
In a daze
I stand fazed
And unaware
Three cold gazes
and one detached stare...
through the looking glass
Yet, I dare
to harness perfection
with the four winds of my directions
A misguided compass...
A soul with no protection
from the elements
Of a harsh winter,
when her streets are flurried
Sent her
Entrepreneurs peddlin'
on the cracks and rocks of concrete
In a hurry
Where
As a child
peddalin'
a bicycle
Was a formidable task
Yet I dare
To love again
To lay in sin
Lie within, the folds of warmth
And familiarity

With clarity,
My vision is obscure
I'm approaching the lure
Of a calloused intimacy
Granted clemency
Left wanting
Haunted
By the daunting task
of
Where to ask
and How to know
Where to stand...
Can,
This girl
Run so far from mistakes
They never catch up
...She constantly aches
Lesions
For all the wrong reasons
Heaving
Commotions
In a closed space
Ocean
Of intense feelings
Sealing the notion
Of simplicity
in this decision,
Heartfelt derision
Finds solace in the comfort
of wanting my necessities
All the while
Simplifying my complexity

VI.

LOVE; The Finale

"YOU LOVE
WITH THE FINALITY OF GRADUATIONS,
THE REALITY THAT THIS IS JUST THE BEGINNING,
THE SPONTANEITY OF SUMMER VACATIONS,
SPRING BREAK MENTALITY,
RELIGIOUS DEVOTION."

Love... Knot

Love...
Will sneak up behind you
Choke you 'till you can't breathe
And step over you when you fall to the ground
It's not that I love not, but the love knots cut off my circulation
And I turn
Pale
And I yearn...for that intimately detached elevation of the systematic sensation of love's stimulation
Of heart
If art... is the medium, my love is the message
That gave birth to the canvas
The copulation of goddesses is, what hands us
Desire...
With the fluidity of my cursive writ penmanship my heart bleeds for love
The pressure was applied...I lied
The original sin was way back when
Those ancient bastards decided to create Aphrodite, Cupid, Eros, and ...
You,
Are the perfect verse over a tight beat
My heads all jumbled and 2 feet stumble,
When I try and walk on the concrete street with a dirt-road-like mentality
Actually, a back alley casualty
Of a cruel game we call Love... the dagger. I possess
While
Attempting to escape your heavenly swagger, hellish aura, angelic smile, earthly torrent, precipitated with all its might
This might
Be defeat
Freezing cold heat, turning January's snow and April's rain to sleet.
Defeat

The embeddedness with which I treaded this, loneliest of lonely streets
And was forced to meet... love
Meanwhile...
Love,
Will make you straddle Him and come...
Rather, arrive at a destination far displaced from resignation
And apprehension
Did I mention, from the back He puts his forearm on your chest and pulls back on your neck real real tight.
He calls that His chokehold
You could fight
If you wanted to
But Love... stops...
Dead in his tracks to tell you, how alive you make Him feel
And revives your train of thought
Motionless, kinda derailment synchronizes the ailment and your "Love sick" kinda tug-at-your-gut Hurt
Dissipates
Now, let's say, I'm not one to hate Hate herself, but Love's always looking for me when I need Him
If Love is an effeminate diety-esque persona then this is just a whim
That in my case, it's a guy
My guy...
And I...
Feel this yearning
Now it's not that I love not, but the love knots...
Make it hurt

Love Transformation

These tears.
This cry is really ugly
The reverse transformation of beauty
Metamorphosis void Kafka
Vision toyed, at last the ... imagery is complete
Butterfly crumpled and contorted, shoved back into its cocoon
Fetus back in womb
Now the clearly distorted rose blossoms before bloom
Full moon sorrow of the caterpillar
Just imagine, the dealer
Of life's cards
Imagine the feeling when life discards
You, Love
You love
With the finality of graduations
The reality that this is just the beginning
The spontaneity of summer vacations
Spring break mentality
Religious devotion
...remind me of the notion, this...
Absolute sincerity
      Honesty, purity, truth
This soul, such an old
                Youth.
We grew, together
She said the weather
Often mirrored her mood
Cumulus cloud stormy attitude
Told me those puzzle pieces were glued
To the cardboard back so they'd stay in place
Backpack lifestyle, we stay in a place
Wet with regrets, hesitant confidings
Memories buried in the hiding
Somewhere
Soul-deep
I wanna say let's keep...   it that way

I mean, um ... lately
It just seems my tears matter a little less
I guess, that's the end result of making this mess
Laying bloody hands all over you
I never knew
I could put everything into trying to be my best for you
He said, "It's kinda hard walking away from a heart you pumped life into"
A chopped down forest grew
One evergreen at a time
Have you ever seen a mind trade places with that beating compass
I'm just, stuttering lately
Butterfly wing fluttering maybe
While encased
Just in case
You leave and I don't get a chance to say TTYL
    "I Love you"...
And you make me smile.
Your laughter's laced with lavender

Love Suicides

Maybe, seeing blood draining'll make the paining less
Than numb
Oil on canvas painting displaying sex success
Turned dumb
Muted speech beseeches
With pleading kisses leading to blisses only dreamt about while apart
While a part of me longs for and misses the kisses of the Mr. (whose Mrs. has the last name of another)
A husband
Has an obligation,
Now with resignation he effaces the mark on my heart, marked as if defacing by the very resigning of the signature signed with permanent ink
Permanent marker
Resignation in my heart, him
The link, a permanent mark on him. Lost art
Searching for the cost, start but's unable to foot the bill
Maybe feet hurrying to pop pills by the bottle
Now, I can't stand, legs shaky wobble
Waddle to see clearly, through blurred vision
Scratched lenses, love you dearly…
Wade through salty water, the Dead Sea of eyes teary,
My mind's weary, its tires screeching to a halt
No one's at fault.
Heart caught, in my throat
Cardiac arrest, straining to see… entreating
With pleading eyes to spare life
Death sentence
Exhibitionists with one witness
You, the ultimate personification of voyeurism
Posing for the camera, created schism
When our angles collide
Last night I died
A thousand little deaths
Caught somewhere between steel bars and labia minora, it wept

Love potion's tears
Branded then seared
This "S" on a chest no longer revered
Solitary confinement of fears
Trapped in picket fences
Amore's death sentences
Mentionin'
Scarlett letter diminishin' the taboo
Now it's become how to... etch my initials in the sands of time
A.   S.
Our hands are tied
We lay on the beach patiently awaiting the tide
But each time the beaches cried, our soaking silhouettes dried
The ebb and flow of life and death
Relentless conditions in, your shore
Sure, mental envisioning of where to carry it out
Scary without
My whole heart
This holed heart
Is leaking blue ink
And the murmurs get louder
I cover your ears
With my fists but the space gets crowdeder
Love shrouded her --- rather our lives
I dives
Headlong with a ball and chain around my waist,
Sinking to a place, anchored in the sand
Grab your hand
And don't let go
All I know
Is I don't know if this is as far as we go
Costumed for show
Our final appearance
Caught with pen and pad, not marked for clearance
Granted clearance to pass that locked gate
Love's fate
Addicted to Valium and his troubles
Sinking equals shrinking air bubbles

Smirking thinking of all the "love you's"
The wear and tear of blinking seeing doubles
When reading one heart
 Strife's existence reminiscent of love struggles
The cyclical battles, tug-of-war
Continuum of pleasure and pain
Your heart has slain
Mine
No apathy in a field of mines
Playing Spades and Dirty Hearts...
Call a Spade a Spade
My heart and mind
         Mind always loses
Time tightens then loosens, this rope around my neck
Better yet, the nooses
On the trees
Bulging eyes no longer see
Through glasses... Strange fruit
Broken glasses, shards and specs
In my windpipe,
                Estranged lover's loot
Fond memories stored in a wreck
And storaged precious moments
First dates, last kisses
Passion's torments
Minutes stolen with reckless abandon
Sexless demandings
Of pleasure
Lost keys, stolen treasures
Lockets in pockets, concoctions measured
To make us sleep...
No more pain... and...
        All the hurt drains……………………….. Slowly.

TWO WORDS ... ONE LOVE

In Love... full of
Sweet smells... sleeps well
Steams seep... dreams keep
      Her mind... her heart
      Her future... her man
      She knows... she owes
      She loves... he sows
His seed... he believes
She believes... one need
Two souls... no weeds
Rose grows... love stems
From them...
EMANATES...PERMEATES...INTEGRATES...
But never...
DISSIPATES...BERATES...DISINTEGRATES
or SEVERS...
              one night... two meals
              no fight... one will
              just right... so still

              Two hearts... one knee
              One art... two see
              No fling... two grasp
              This thing... called LOVE
              They cry... then hug
              No sigh... no shrug

One proposal...
Thinking...
              Not blinking... just winking
              She's shrinking, and shaking
              And pinching... not waking
              No flinching... not dreaming
                    He's beaming... and scared
                    He's seeing... her there

                    "Just say you will
                    I pray you will
                    One day we will..."

    One day...
            One bride...One groom
    Will say...
            "I Do"...
    One day
        ...TWO WORDS ONE LOVE...

www.ingramcontent.com/pod-product-compliance
Lightning Source LLC
Chambersburg PA
CBHW031205090426
42736CB00009B/792